THE TRAGEDY
OF
WHITE INJUSTICE

By Marcus Garvey

978-1-63923-076-1

All Rights reserved. No part of this book maybe reproduced without written permission from
the publishers, except by a reviewer who may quote brief passages in a review to be printed in a newspaper or magazine.

Printed August, 2021

Cover Art By: Paul Amid

Published and Distributed By:
Lushena Books
607 Country Club Drive, Unit E
Bensenville, IL 60106
www.lushenabks.com

ISBN: 978-1-63923-076-1

Printed in the United States of America

FOREWORD.

BECAUSE of the circumstances of time, it is thought that the re-presentation of this little pamphlet would not be amiss in somewhat achieving the original object that it was designed to accomplish—that of giving the Negro a thought, with the hope of inspiring him toward the freeing of himself from the ugly octopus of race prejudice and exploitation, which has been devouring him in his universal association with certain members of the white race.

All good psychologists realize that if you can set a man thinking you are likely to produce, through him, results that never would have been possible otherwise. The object I have in view is to get the Negro to accomplish much for himself out of his own thoughtfulness. To arouse that thoughtfulness, he must be shocked or otherwise he must be driven to see the unusual that is operating against him, and so this little pamphlet was written during a time of leisure in jail in 1927, in the peculiar form in which it appears. It is not verse, neither is it orthodox prose, but it is a kind of mean adopted for the purpose of conveying the desired thought.

The first and second editions of this pamphlet were published in the United States by Mrs. Amy Jacques Garvey, whilst I was doing a five-year sentence at Atlanta, Ga., as the result of the white man's prejudice in America, and thousands of copies have been circulated all over the world. There has been constant demand for more copies, but it has just been found convenient to publish the third edition. This was chiefly inspired by the present war conditions, where another section of the white race—the Italians, under their mad leader, Mussolini—has seen it customarily proper, to again invade free African territory. Following the course of the old land thieves, Mussolini has organized an unusual savagelike military outfit to conquer Abyssinia, the avowed purpose being to afford Italy economic and political expansion, disregarding all the rights of the Abyssinians to the peaceful possession of their native land. It is evident, therefore, that some of the white race have not changed much during the centuries. They are still barbarous, savage, and in every way inhuman and unjust. The war in Abyssinia proves their modern barbarism and savagery, hence, no one may say that what is contained in this little pamphlet is not really true of the character and disposition of the white man in his association with the weaker, and particularly the darker peoples of the world. Probably, if he reads this he himself may get a conscious thought in realizing how unworthy is his character as is shown by his conduct among other people. If it could achieve no other good than that of making him realize how unworthy he is of being a real human being, and more so a Christian, the publication would not have been in vain. It must be remembered that this is not an attempt at poetry: it is just a peculiar style of using facts as they impress me as I go through the pages of history and as I look at and note the conduct of the white race.

MARCUS GARVEY.

2, Beaumont Crescent,
   West Kensington, London, W.14.
      England.

November, 1935.

(1)

Lying and stealing is the whiteman's game;
For rights of God nor man he has no shame
(A practice of his throughout the whole world)
At all, great thunderbolts he has hurled;
He has stolen everywhere—land and sea;
A buccaneer and pirate he must be,
Killing all, as he roams from place to place,
Leaving disease, mongrels—moral disgrace.

(2)

The world's history of him is replete,
From his javelin-bolt to new-built fleet:
Hosts he has robbed and crushed below;
Of friend and neighbour he has made a foe.
From our men and women he made the slave,
Then boastingly he calls himself a brave;
Cowardly, he steals on his trusting prey,
Killing in the dark, then shouts he hoo ray !

(3)

Not to go back to time pre-historic,
Only when men in Nature used to frolic,
And you will find his big, long murder-list,
Showing the plunderings of his mailed fist;
Africa, Asia and America
Tell the tale in a mournful replica
How tribesmen, Indians and Zulus fell
Fleeing the murdering bandit pell mell.

(4)

American Indian tribes were free,
Sporting, dancing, and happy as could be;
Asia's hordes lived then a life their own,
To civilization they would have grown;
Africa's millions laughed with the sun,
In the cycle of man a course to run;
In stepped the white man, bloody and grim,
The light of these people's freedom to dim.

4

(5)

Coolies of Asiatics they quickly made,
In Africa's blacks they built a world trade,
The Red Indians they killed with the gun,
All else of men and beasts they put to run;
Blood of murderer Cain is on their head,
Of man and beast they mean to kill,—dead;
A world of their own is their greatest aim,
For which Yellow and Black are well to blame.

(6)

Out of cold old Europe these white men came,
From caves, dens and holes, without any fame,
Eating their dead's flesh and sucking their blood,
Relics of the Mediterranean flood;
Literature, science and art they stole,
After Africa had measured each pole,
Asia taught them what great learning was,
Now they frown upon what the Coolie does.

(7)

They have stolen, murdered, on their way here,
Leaving desolation and waste everywhere;
Now they boastingly tell what they have done,
Seeing not the bloody crown they have won;
Millions of Blacks died in America,
Coolies, peons, serfs, too, in Asia;
Upon these dead bones Empires they builded,
Parceling out crowns and coronets gilded.

(8)

Trifling with God's Holy Names and Law,
Mixing Christ's religion that had no flaw,
They have dared to tell us what is right,
In language of death-bullets, gas and might.
Only with their brute force they hold us down,
Men of colour, Yellow, Red, Black and Brown:
Not a fair chance give they our men to rise.
Christian liars we see in their eyes.

(9)

With the Bible they go to foreign lands,
Taking Christ and stealth in different hands;
Making of God a mockery on earth,
When of the Holy One there is no dearth:
They say to us: " You, sirs, are the heathen,
" We your brethren—Christian fellowmen,
" We come to tell the story of our God ";
When we believe, they give to us the rod.

(10)

After our confidence they have thus won,
From our dear land and treasures we must run:
Story of the Bible no more they tell,
For our souls redeemed we could go to hell.
Oil, coal and rubber, silver and gold,
They have found in wealth of our lands untold;
Thus, they claim the name of our country—all:
Of us they make then their real foot-ball.

(11)

If in the land we happen to tarry,
Most of us then become sad and sorry,
For a white man's country they say it is,
And with shot, gas and shell, they prove it his:
What can we do who love the Gracious Lord,
But fight, pray, watch and wait His Holy word:
His second coming we know to be true,
Then, He will greet the white man with his due.

(12)

This Christ they killed on Calvary's Cross,
After His Person around they did toss:
White men the Saviour did crucify,
For eyes not blue, but blood of Negro tie;
Now they worship Him in their churches great,
And of the Holy Ghost they daily prate;
" One God " they say, enough for all mankind,
When in slavery the Blacks they entwined.

6

(13)

Their churches lines of demarcation draw;
In the name of Christ there is no such law,
Yet Black and White they have separated,
A Jim Crow God the preachers operated,
Then to Heaven they think they will all go,
When their consciences ought to tell them NO.
God is no respecter of persons great,
So each man must abide his final fate.

(14)

We'd like to see the white man converted,
And to right and justice be devoted;
Continuing in land-values to lie and steal,
Will bring destruction down upon his heel.
All that the other races want, I see,
Is the right to liberty and be free;
This the selfish white man doesn't want to give;
He alone, he thinks, has the right to live.

(15)

There shall be a bloody mix-up everywhere;
Of the white man's plunder we are aware:
Men of colour the great cause understand,
Unite they must, to protect their own land.
No fool's stand on argument must we make;
Between Heaven and earth an oath we take:
" Our lands to deliver from foreign foes,
Caring not of trials and maudlin woes."

(16)

The privilege of men to protect home
Was established before the days of Rome.
Many gallant races fought and died,
Alien hordes in triumph thus defied.
Carthage did not crush Ancient Greece
For their believing in the Golden Fleece.
No other race shall kill the sturdy Blacks
If on their tribal gods we turn our backs.

(17)

From Marathon, Tours, Blenheim and the Marne
A braver courage in man has been born;
Africans died at Thermopylae's Pass,
Standing firm for Persia—men of Brass.
The Black Archers of Ethiopia stood
At Marathon, proving their stern manhood;
Senegalese held their own at Verdun,
Even though their praises are not now sung.

(18)

In the Americas' modern warfare
The Blacks have ever borne their share;
With Cortez, Washington, too, and the rest,
We did for the others our truthful best;
At St. Domingo we struck a clear blow
To show which way the wind may one day go.
Toussaint L'Ouverture was our leader then,
At the time when we were only half-men.

(19)

Italians, Menclik put to chase,
Beating a retreat in uneven haste;
So down the line of history we come,
Black, courtly, courageous and handsome.
No fear have we to-day of any great man
From Napoleon back to Genghis Khan;
All we ask of men is " Give a square deal,"
Returning to others same right we feel.

(20)

With a past brilliant, noble and grand,
Black men march to the future hand in hand;
We have suffered long from the white man's greed,
Perforce he must change his unholy creed.
Stealing, bullying and lying to all
Will drag him to ignominious fall;
For men are wise—yes, no longer are fools,
To have grafters make of them still cheap tools.

B

(21)

Each race should be proud and stick to its own,
And the best of what they are should be shown;
This is no shallow song of hate to sing,
But over Blacks there should be no white king.
Every man on his own foothold should stand,
Claiming a nation and a Fatherland.
White, Yellow and Black should make their own laws,
And force no one-sided justice with flaws.

(22)

Man will bear so much of imposition,
Till he starts a righteous inquisition.
History teaches this as a true fact,
Upon this premise all men do act.
Sooner or later each people take their stand
To fight against the strong, oppressive hand;
This is God's plan, raising man to power,
As over sin and greed He makes him tower.

(23)

This trite lesson the white man has not learnt,
Waiting until he gets his fingers burnt.
Milleniums ago, when white men slept,
The great torch of light Asia kept.
Africa at various periods shone
Above them all as the bright noonday sun;
Coming from the darkened cave and hut,
The white man opened the gate that was shut.

(24)

Gradually light bore down upon him,
This ancient savage who was once dim;
When he commenced to see and move around,
He found the book of knowledge on the ground;
Centuries of wonder and achievements
Were cast before him in God's compliments;
But, like the rest, he has now fallen flat,
And must in the Lord's cycle yield for that.

(25)

We shall always be our brother's keeper,
Is the injunction of the Redeemer;
Love and tolerance we must ever show,
If in Grace Divine we would truly grow:
This is the way clear to God's great kingdom—
Not by the death-traps of Argonne or Somme,
When the terrible white man learns this much,
He will save even the African Dutch.

(26)

South Africa has a grave problem now
In reducing the Negro to the plow;
White men are to live in their lazy ease,
While the patience of the goodly natives tease;
They make new laws to have Africa white
Precipitating righteous and ready fight:
Around the world they speak of being so just,
Yet, in fact, no lone white man can you trust.

(27)

In Australia the same they have done,
And so, wherever man's confidence won:
This they call the religion of the Christ,
And upon their willing slave try to foist.
Only a part of the world may you fool,
And easily reduce to your foot-stool;
The other one-half is always awake,
And from it you cannot liberty take.

(28)

" And now valiant Black men of the west
Must ably rise to lead and save the rest " :
This is the ringing call Africa sounds,
As throughout the Godly world it resounds;
Clansmen ! black, educated, virile and true !
Let us prove too that we are loyal blue.
We must win in the blessed fight of love,
Trusting on the Maker of men above.

10

(29)

The Christian world is yet to be saved!
Man, since the risen Christ has not behaved!
Wanton, reckless, wicked, he still remains,
Causing grief, sorrow, tears and human pains!
Can we show the Godly light to anyone
Seeking for earnest truth while marching on?
If so, friend, let us tell you now and here,
For love, freedom, justice, let's all prepare!

(30)

God in His Glorious Might is coming,
Wonderful signs He is ever showing,
Unrest, earthquakes, hurricanes, floods and storms
Are but revelations of Heavenly Forms:
The proud white scientist thinks he is wise
But the Black man's God comes in true disguise,
God is sure in the rumbling earthquake,
When He is ready, the whole world will shake.

(31)

The Armageddon is gathering now;
The sign is on every oppressed man's brow:
The whites who think they are ever so smart
Do not know other men can play their part:
When the opportune time is almost here
Black, Yellow and Brown will be ev'rywhere,
In union of cause they'll stand together,
And storms of the bully boldly weather.

(32)

Their gases and shots, and their rays of death,
Shall only be child's play—a dream of Seth,
For out of the clear, sleeping minds of ages,
Wonders shall be written on history's pages:
Our buried arts and sciences then shall rise,
To show how for centuries we were wise:
Silent tongues we kept, by God's true command,
Until of us, action, He did demand.

11

(33)

Under the canopy of Nature's law
We shall unitedly and bravely draw,
On the plains of God's green Amphitheatre,
Swords, in rhythm with Divine Meter:
Jehovah's Day will have surely come,
With Angelic strains and Seraphic hum:
The Guides of Heaven will direct the way,
Keeping us from wandering far astray.

(34)

Like around the high walls of Jericho,
March we, as Rio speeds through Mexico:
Trumpets loud will the Guiding Angels blow,
As scatter the enemy to-and-fro:
Heaven will have given us a battle cry:
" Oh Brave Soldiers you shall never die ":
Rally to the command of Heaven's King,
As Cherubim to Him your tidings bring.

(35)

See the deadly clash of arms! Watch! They fall!
There is stillness!—It is the funeral pall!
A sad requiem now is to be sung,—
Not by Angels, but in their human tongue!
The cruel masters of yest'rday are done!
From the fields of battle they have run!
A brand new world of justice is to be,—
" You shall be a true brother unto me! "

(36)

This is a forecast of God's wrath:
White man, will you turn from the evil path?
There is still hope for you, among the good.
If you will seek the bigger-brotherhood:
Stop your tricks, frauds, lying and stealing,
And settle down to fair and square dealing;
If not, prepare yourself for gloomy hell,
As God announces the sorrowing knell.

(37)

Your lies, to us called diplomacy,
Are known by us, a brazen phantasy;
You imprison men for crimes not so great,
While on your silly wisdom you do prate.
The masses are soberly watching you;
They know that you are false and so untrue.
The labourers of your race you oppress,
As well as black and other men you distress.

(38)

If you were wise you'd read between the lines
Of feudal " isms " and others of old times.
Men have fought against ugly royal gods,
Burying them 'neath European sods.
Such to heartless masters the people do,
From Syracuse to bloody Waterloo;
Wonderful lessons for any sober man,
Who worships not idols or the god of Pan.

(39)

In the vicious order of things to-day,
The poor, suffering black man has no say:
The plot is set for one 'gainst the other,
With organization they mustn't bother.
" If one should show his head as a leader,
Whom we cannot use, the rest to pilfer,
We shall discredit him before his own,
And make of him a notorious clown."

(40)

" In Africa we have plans to watch him,
While the native Chiefs of their lands we trim;
The Blacks schooled in England are too smart,
On the I BETTER THAN YOU scheme we'll start,
And have them thinking away from the rest;
This philosophy for them is best—
Easier then we can rob the good lands
And make ourselves rich without soiled hands."

18

(41)

" We will so keep from them the ' NEGRO
    WORLD '
That no news they'll have of a flag unfurled;
Should they smuggle copies in, and we fail,
We will send the sly agents all to jail."
This is the white man's plan across the sea.
Isn't this wily and vicious as can be?
In other lands they have things arranged
Differently, yet they have never changed.

(42)

In America they have Coloured to tell
What they know of the rest, whose rights they sell;
The Blacks they do try to keep always down,
But in time they will reap what they have sown.
No Negro's good life is safe in the STATES
If he tries to be honest with his mates;
In politics he must sell at the polls,
To suit the white man in his many roles.

(43)

The West Indian whites are tricky, too;
They have schemes curved like the horse's shoe:
There is only one opening for the black—
Three other sides are close up to his back;
Hence he never gets a chance to look in
Whilst staring at the world of mortal sin.
Yes, this is the game they play everywhere,
Leaving the Negro to gloom and despair.

(44)

And now, white man, can we reason with you,
For each race in the world to give its due?
Africa for Africans is most right;
Asia for Asiatics is light;
To Europe for the Europeans,
America for the Americans :
This is the doctrine of the goodly Klan.
Now fighting for the alien ban.

14

(45)

Blacks do not hate you because you are white;
We believe in giving to all men right;
Some we do keep for ourselves to protect,
Knowing it as a virtue to select.
We are willing to be friends of mankind,
Pulling all together with none behind,
Growing in sane goodness and fellowship,
Choosing but the Almighty to worship.

(46)

Let justice prevail, at home and abroad;
Cease over the weak your burdens to lord;
You're but mortal man, like the rest of us—
Of this happy truth we need make no fuss.
All Nature's kindly gifts are justly ours—
Suns, oceans, trees, to pretty flowers—
So we need not doubt the marvellous fact
That God has given to each man his tract.

(47)

The common thief now steals a crust of bread,
The law comes down upon his hungry head;
The haughty land robber steals continents,
With men, oil, gold, rubber and all contents.
The first you say is a hopeless convic',
While the latter escapes the law by trick;
That grave, one-sided justice will not do—
The poor call for consideration, too.

(48)

The rich white man starts the unholy war,
Then from the line of action he keeps far;
He pushes to the front sons of the poor,
There to do battle, die, suffer galore.
As the guns rage, liberty loans they raise,
And in glorious tones sing freedom's praise.
This is the method to gain them more wealth,
Then, after vict'ry they practice great stealth.

(49)

Those who make wars should first go to the front,
And of gas, shot and shell bear there the brunt;
In first lines of action they are all due,
If to their country and people they are true:
When this is demanded in right of all,
There will be no more deadly cannon ball:
The downtrodden poor whites and blacks should join
And prevent rich whites our rights to purloin.

(50)

Weeping mothers, tricked in patriotism,
Send their sons to fight for liberalism:
Into most far off lands they go with pride,
Thinking right and God be on their side:
When they get into the bloody trenches,
They find of lies they had awful-drenches:
The people they were all supposed to kill,
Like themselves, had gotten of lies their fill.

(51)

In the private club and drawing room,
White schemes are hatched for the nation's doom:
Speculators, grafters, bankers—all,
With politicians join to hasten the fall,
By stealing rights from other citizens,
As if they weren't fit or true denizens:
How awful is this daring story
That we tell to men young and hoary.

(52)

Crooked lawyers, friends and politicians,
Corrupt the morals of the good nations:
Between them and others, fly plots they make,
Innocent citizens' money to take:
From banks they find out your real account,
Then have you indicted on legal count:
Large fees they charge, to have you surely broke,
Then, to prison you go—what a sad joke!

(53)

The white man controls cable and wireless,
Connections by ships with force and duress :
He keeps black races of the world apart,
So to his schemes they may not be smart :
" There shall be no Black Star Line Ships," he says,
" For that will interfere with our crooked ways :
" I'll disrupt their business and all their plans,
" So they might not connect with foreign lands."

(54)

Black women are raped by the lordly white,
In colonies, the shame ne'er reaching light :
In other countries abuses are given,
Shocking to morality and God's Heaven.
Hybrids and mongrels are the open result,
Which the whites give us as shameful insult :
How can they justify this ?   None can tell;
Yet, crimes of the blacks are rung with a bell.

(55)

White men newspapers subsidize and own,
For to keep them on their racial throne :
Editors are slaves to fool the public,
Reporters tell the lie and pull the trick ;
The papers support only what they want,
Yet truth, fair play, and justice, daily flaunt :
They make criminals out of honest men,
And force judges to send them to the Pen.

(56)

Capitalists buy up all blank space
To advertise and hold the leading place
For to influence public opinion
And o'er Chief-editors show dominion.
The average man is not wise to the scheme,
He, the reformer, must now redeem ;
This isn't a smooth or very easy job,
For, you, of your honour and name, they'll rob.

17

(57)

The bankers employ men to shoot and kill,
When we interfere with their august will;
They take the savings of deaf, dumb and poor,
Gamble with it here and on foreign shore:
In oil, gold, rum, rubber they speculate,
Then bring their foreign troubles upon the State:
Friends in Government they control at will;
War they make, for others, our sons to kill.

(58)

The many foundations of researches,
And the foreign missions and their churches,
Are organized to catch the mild converts
Who don't understand the way of perverts.
Our wealth when discovered by researchers,
In lands of the Native occupiers
Is surveyed and marked to the river's rim
Till they dislodge a Premprey or Abd-El-Krim.

(59)

It is not freedom from prison we seek;
It is freedom from the big Christian freak:
All life is now a soulless prison cell,
A wild suspense between heaven and hell:
Selfish, wicked whites have made it so;
To the Author and Finisher we'll go,
Carrying our sad cares and many wrongs
To Him in prayers and holy songs.

(60)

This is the game that is played all around,
Which is, sure, one day, to each race rebound:
The world is gone mad with the money craze,
Leaving the poor man in a gloomy haze:
There must be world reorganization,
To save the masses from exploitation:
The cry is for greater democracy,
A salvation from man's hypocrisy.

18

(61)

Out in this heartless, bitter oasis,
There's now very little of human bliss;
The cold capitalists and money sharks
Have made life unsafe, like ocean barks
The once dear, lovely Garden of Eden
Has become the sphere of men uneven;
The good God created but an equal pair,
Now man has robbed others of their share.

(62)

Shall there be freedom of liberal thought?
No; the white man has all agencies bought—
Press, pulpit, law and every other thing—
Hence o'er public opinion he reigns king.
This is indisputable, glaring fact;
You may find it out with a little tact.
College tutors and presidents are paid,
So that in universities schemes are laid

(63)

Cleopatra, Empress Josephine,
Were black mongrels like of the Philippine :—
Mixtures from black and other races they,—
Yet, " true," the white man's history will not say
To those who seek the light of pure knowledge
In the inquiring world, school or college.
Napoleon fell for a Negro woman;
So did the Caesars, and the Great Roman.

(64)

Anthony lost his imperial crown
To escape Cleo's fascinating frown.
This truth the New Negro knows very well,
And to his brothers in darkness he'll tell.
No one can imprison the brain of man—
That was never intended in God's plan;
You may persecute, starve, even debase—
That will not kill truth nor virtue efface.

19

(65)

The white man now enjoys his " Vanity Fair ";
He thinks of self and not of others care—
Fratricidal course, that to hell doth lead—
This is poison upon which the gentry feed.
Blacks should study physics, chemistry, more,
While the " gold god " all such sinners adore;
This is no idle prattle talk to you;
It has made the banners red, white and blue.

(66)

Out of the clear of God's Eternity
Shall rise a kingdom of Black Fraternity;
There shall be conquests o'er militant forces;
For as man proposes, God disposes.
Signs of retribution are on every hand:
Be ready, black men, like Gideon's band.
They may scoff and mock at you to-day,
But get you ready for the awful fray.

(67)

In the fair movement of God's Abounding Grace
There is a promised hope for the Negro race;
In the sublimest truth of prophecy,
God is to raise them to earthly majesty.
Princes shall come out of Egypt so grand,
The noble black man's home and Motherland,
The Psalmist spoke in holy language clear,
As Almighty God's Triune will declare.

(68)

In their conceit they see not their ruin;
You soldiers of trust, be up and doing!
Remember Belshazzar's last joyous feast,
And Daniel's vision of the Great Beast!
" Weighed in the balances and found wanting "
Is the Tekel to which they are pointing.
This interpretation of the Prophet
Black men shall never in their dreams forget.

The resplendent rays of the morning sun
Shall kiss the Negro's life again begun;
The music of God's rhythmic natural law
Shall stir Afric's soul without Divine flaw.
The perfume from Nature's rosy hilltops
Shall fall on us, spiritual dewdrops.
Celestial beings shall know us well,
For, by goodness, in death, with them we'll dwell.

AND HOW SAD A FINIS!

With battleship, artillery and gun
White men have put all God's creatures to run;
Heaven and earth they have often defied,
Taking no heed of the rebels that died.
God can't be mocked in this daring way,
So the evil ones shall sure have their day.
" You may rob, you may kill, for great fame,"
So says the white man, FOR THIS IS HIS GAME.

Hail! United States of Africa!

Hail! United States of Africa—free!
Hail! Motherland most bright, divinely fair!
State in perfect sisterhood united,
Born in truth; mighty thou shalt ever be.

Hail! Sweet land of our father's noble kin!
Let joy within thy bounds be ever known;
Friend of the wandering poor, and helpless, thou,
Light to all, such as freedom's, reigns within.

From Liberia's peaceful western coast
To the foaming Cape at the southern end,
There's but one law and sentiment sublime,
One flag, and its emblem of which we boast.

The Nigerias are all united now,
Sierra Leone and the Gold Coast, too.
Gambia, Senegal, not divided,
But in one union happily bow

The treason of the centuries is dead,
All alien whites are forever gone;
The glad home of Sheba is once more free,
As o'er the world the black man raised his head.

Bechuanaland, a State with Kenya,
Members of the Federal Union grand,
Send their greetings to sister Zanzibar,
And so does laughing Tanganyika.

Over in Grand Mother Mozambique,
The pretty Union Flag floats in the air,
She is sister to good Somaliland,
Smiling with the children of Dahomey.

Three lusty cheers for old Basutoland,
Timbuctoo, Tunis and Algeria,
Uganda, Kamerun, all together
Are in the union with Nyasaland.

ve waited long for fiery Morocco,
Now with Guinea and Togo she has come,
All free and equal in the sisterhood,
Like Swazi, Zululand and the Congo.

There is no state left out of the Union—
The East, West, North, South, including Central,
Are in the nation, strong forever,
Over blacks in glorious dominion.

Hail! United States of Africa—free!
Country of the brave black man's liberty;
State of greater nationhood thou has won,
A new life for the race is just begun.

Africa for the Africans

Say! Africa for the Africans,
Like America for the Americans:
This the rallying cry for a nation,
Be it in peace or revolution.

Blacks are men, no longer cringing fools;
They demand a place, not like weak tools;
But among the world of nations great
They demand a free self-governing state.

Hurrah! Hurrah! Great Africa wakes;
She is calling her sons, and none forsakes,
But to colours of the nation runs,
Even though assailed by enemy guns.

Cry it loud, and shout it long, hurrah!
Time has changed, so hail! New Africa!
We are now awakened, rights to see;
We shall fight for dearest liberty.

Mighty kingdoms have been truly reared
On the bones of blackmen, facts declared;
History tells this awful, pungent truth,
Africa awakes to her rights forsooth.

Europe cries to Europeans, ho!
Asiatics claim Asia, so
Australia for Australians,
And Africa for the Africans.

Blackmen's hands have joined now together,
They will fight and brave all death's weather,
Motherland to save, and make her free,
Spreading joy for all to live and see.

None shall turn us back, in freedom's name,
We go marching like to men of fame
Who have given laws and codes to kings,
Sending evil flying on crippled wings.

Blackmen shall in groups reassemble,
Rich and poor and the great and humble:
Justice shall be their rallying cry,
When millions of soldiers pass us by.

Look for that day, coming, surely soon,
When the sons of Ham will show no Coon
Could the mighty deeds of valour do
Which shall bring giants for peace to sue.

Hurrah! Hurrah! Better times are near;
Let us front the conflict and prepare;
Greet the world as soldiers, bravely true:
" Sunder not," Africa shouts to you.

www.ingramcontent.com/pod-product-compliance
Lightning Source LLC
Chambersburg PA
CBHW060608030426
42337CB00019B/3663